THE FIFTIES

Editors: William Duffy, Robert Bly

Second Issue   1959

POEMS OF GOTTFRIED BENN	2
THE WORK OF ROBERT CREELEY 　　　　　　　—CRUNK	10
A NOTE ON SYLLABICS	22
POEMS OF JUAN RAMÓN JIMÉNEZ	24
REPLY TO CECIL HEMLEY 　　　　　—WILLIAM DUFFY	34
THE POSSIBILITY OF NEW POETRY	36
A PARAGRAPH OF VALÉRY	37
AMERICAN POEMS 　　JAMES WRIGHT 　　ROBERT BLY 　　THOMAS PARNELL	38
SOME NEW BOOKS	44
ON ENGLISH AND AMERICAN POETRY 　　　　　—ROBERT BLY	45
MADAME TUSSAUD'S WAX MUSEUM	48
WISDOM OF THE OLD	50
CONTRIBUTORS	53

THE FIFTIES is published quarterly by The Fifties, Briarwood Hill, Pine Island, Minnesota. Subscriptions $2.00 per year in the U.S. and Canada; foreign $2.50. Single copy $.50. Manuscripts will not be returned unless accompanied by stamped, self-addressed envelopes. Payment: $10.00 per page for poems and translations of poems; $7.50 per page for prose. Printed by The Kerryman Ltd., Tralee, Ireland.

Reprint by Hobart & William Smith
College Press in Association
with the Seneca Review
Geneva, New York 14456

REPRINT BY PERMISSION
OF THE EDITOR

GOTTFRIED BENN

ACH; DAS FERNE LAND

Ach, das ferne Land,
wo das Herzzereissende
auf runden Kiesel
oder Schilffläche libellenflüchtig
anmurmelt,
auch der Mond
verschlagenen Lichts
—halb Reif, halb Ährenweiss—
den Doppelgrund der Nacht
so tröstlich anhebt—

ach, das ferne Land,
wo vom Schimmer der See'n
die Hügel warm sind,
zum Beispiel Asolo, wo die Duse ruht,
von Pittsburg trug sie der 'Duilio' heim,
alle Kriegschiffe, auch die englischen, flaggten
                              halbmast,
also er Gibraltar passierte—

dort Selbstgespräche
ohne Beziehungen auf Nahes,
Selbstgefühle,
frühe Mechanismen,
Totemfragmente
in die weiche Luft—
etwas Rosinenbrot im Rock—,
so fallen die Tage,
bis der Ast am Himmel steht,
auf dem die Vögel einruhn
nach langem Flug.

GOTTFRIED BENN

GOTTFRIED BENN

AH, THAT LAND SO FAR OFF

Ah, that land so far off,
where the heart-breaking sea
on round pebbles
or rushy land quick as a dragon-fly
continues to murmur,
also the crafty
light of the moon
—half frosty, half white as an ear of grain—
lifts so consolingly
the double depth of the night—

ah, that land so far off,
where the hills, from the shimmer
of the sea, are warm,
Asolo, for instance, where Duse lies,
'Duilio' carried her home from Pittsburgh,
all warships, even the English, flags at half-mast
as he passed Gibraltar—

There are long speeches with oneself,
without bearing on what is near us,
self-absorption,
primitive mechanisms,
remains of taboo
in the soft air,
some raisin-bread in the coat pocket—
so the days fall,
until the bough stands bare against the heaven,
on which birds stop to rest
on their long journey.

From Statische Gedichte,
translated by Robert Bly.

STATISCHE GEDICHTE

Entwicklungsfremdheit
ist die Tiefe des Weisen,
Kinder und Kindeskinder
beunruhigen ihn nicht,
dringen nicht in ihn ein.

Richtungen vertreten,
Handeln,
Zu- und Abreisen
ist das Zeichen einer Welt,
die nicht klar sieht.
Vor meinem Fenster,
—sagt der Weise—
leigt ein Tal,
darin sammeln sich die Schatten,
zwei Pappeln säumen einen Weg,
due weisst—wohin.

Perspektivismus
ist ein anderes Wort für seine Statik:
Linien anlegen,
sie weiterführen
nach Rankengesetz—,
Ranken sprühen—,
auch Schwärme, Krähen,
auswerfen in Winterrot von Frühhimmeln,

dann sinken lassen—,

du weisst—für wen.

POEMS THAT STAND STILL

A coolness to the coming of generations
is the depth of the Wise Man,
children and the children of children
do not bring him unrest,
do not pierce him.

To represent some party,
Busyness,
Travelling to, and from,
is the distinguishing stamp of a world
which does not see well.
Before my window,
the Wise Man said,
a valley lies,
the shadows gather together there,
two poplars show a road,
you know—where.

Perspective
is another word for his way of standing still:
to mark down lines,
the lines grow farther on
according to the laws of plants which put out shoots—
Jungle plants throw out shoots—
multitudes of birds also, crows
thrown out in winter dawn from early heaven—

then to allow them all to sink—

you know—for whom.

From Statische Gedichte
translated by Robert Bly.

LEBE WOHL

Lebe wohl, du Flüchtige, Freie
die Flügel zu Fahrt und Flug—
geschlossen die Rune, die Reihe,
die deinen Namen trug.

Ich muss nun wieder
meine dunklen Gärten begehn,
ich höre schon Schwanenlieder
vom Schilf der nächtigen Seen.

Lebe wohl, du Tränenbereiter,
Erröfner von Qual und Gram,
verloren—weiter
die Tiefe, die gab und nahm.

FAREWELL—

Farewell, you fugitive thing, free
Your wings for journey and flight—
The runes and the rows are finished
Which carried your name.

I must now traverse
My dark gardens again,
I hear already the songs of swans
From the sedge of the nightly seas.

Farewell, you supplier of tears,
Amasser of torment and grief,
Lost—farther on
Are the depths, which gave and took away.

From Gesammelte Gedichte,
Limes-Verlag, Wiesbaden, 1956,
translated by Edith DeSort.

THE WORK OF ROBERT CREELEY

WE THINK OF THE MODERN tradition as being indivisible, like water, but actually there are seven or eight strong traditions within the modern tradition, and a poet may have the strength and courage to participate in one or more of those traditions. It is obvious to everyone that Robert Creeley has some courage.

The work of Robert Creeley includes, I think, not only his poems, but also his work for the Black Mountain group; this group, to which he has devoted so much time, is perhaps for the first time in America, nearly a 'school', in the French sense. Their work has made the *Black Mountain Review*, of which Mr. Creeley is the editor, an honest and intelligent review, and in some ways the most interesting magazine in America. The group includes Charles Olson, an American from New England, in Lowell's generation, who among other things wrote the book on Melville which Grove Press has published; Irving Layton, a Canadian in the same generation; Robert Duncan, now increasingly admired, also in the generation of the Forties; and others, both older, such as Louis Zukofsky, the old radical, who is still writing on, and younger, such as Denise Levertov.

The poems of these poets have appeared regularly in the *Black Mountain Review*, in Cid Corman's *Origin*, certain California quarterlies, and of the more national magazines, only in *Poetry Magazine*, which has made an effort to represent them. The book publisher for this group has been, for the most part, Jonathan Williams, a young man in Highlands, North Carolina, who supports the press on his own income, has the books printed in various countries of the world, and has printed since he started in 1951 about thirty-five books. That is a lot of work. He published in 1953 Creeley's *The Immoral Proposition* and in 1955 *All That Is Lovely In Men*, both now out of print, and in 1957 *The Whip*; and he also publishes the *Black Mountain Review*, which is now up to #8. Mr. Creeley has also published four other books elsewhere: *Le Fou*, Golden Goose Press in 1952, *The Kind of Act Of*, Divers Press in 1953, *The Gold Diggers* (short stories), Divers Press, 1954, and *If You*, Porpoise Bookshop, San Francisco, in 1956. The most available book of Mr. Creeley's is *The Whip*, a small book of selected poems, from which the poems quoted in this review are taken. This book, at $1.00, is available from the Phoenix Book Store, 14 Cornelia St., N.Y., or from Mr. Williams himself at Highlands, North Carolina. As Mr. Williams mentions somewhere, magazines such as the *Kenyon Review*, the *Partisan Review*, *The Nation*, *The New Republic*, and *The Saturday Review* have yet to review one of Mr. Williams' thirty-five books, but they are reviewed frequently in *Poetry Magazine* and occasionally in the *New York Times*.

The books of poems by men in this group occasionally have introductions by William Carlos Williams, whom they admire both for his long and independent creative life, and his rugged 'local' quality. I know none of these men, but I gather they also respect Pound, not only for his daring of mind, and freedom from the old Georgian cant, but also for his continual hard-headed insistence that all is not well in America, this best of all possible worlds.

These poets are somehow politically more mature than the usual poet in, for instance, *Poetry Magazine*, and understand that some form of oppression today, even in America, is as common as beauty, for those who have senses which can grasp it. And they are all ornery men. If total oppression came, a poet like Robert Hillyer would probably become Poet Laureate, and these men, not formidable so much as ornery, would probably be shot instantly to keep them out of trouble. And that is some sort of compliment.

It must be said for William Carlos Williams that he has a kind of vitality which inspires a considerable amount of thought in younger men; in other words, he has disciples, and that certainly cannot be said for such men as Eliot or Jeffers or Tate, or even such a fine poet as Marianne Moore. We remember that the sources of the recent activity in San Francisco, namely Allen Ginsberg and Jack Kerouac, both profess also a strange relationship to William Carlos Williams, who in this case acts as a sort of windowpane, behind which they see Whitman, who is temperamentally much more unapproachable. With this common devotion to William Carlos Williams, we should not be surprised to see these men appearing in Robert Creeley's magazine. In fact, Ginsberg's best poem, *America*, was first published there, and later, other San Francisco people have appeared in the *Black Mountain*, including Gary Snyder, and the good short-story writer, Michael Rumaker. Mr. Rexroth was also, several years ago, connected with the magazine.

In other words, this is an amorphous group, having in common a respect of William Carlos Williams and Ezra Pound, an interest in independent thought, a dislike of hacks and innocents, and what is perhaps not so healthy, a sort of American isolationism.

There is an anecdote about Yeats and Sandburg. Yeats was making one of his lecture and reading tours of America, about 1912, and he came to Chicago, I suppose in some connection with Harriet Monroe. After reading many poems on Irish themes, and perhaps, telling a few anecdotes of literary life in London, it seems Mr. Sandburg stood up and asked in an angry voice why, if Yeats was an Irishman, he did not live and write in his own country instead of in a foreign one? Mr. Yeats replied that Paris was the center of the world of poetry, but unfortunately he could not speak French; so he lived as close to Paris as a man could who could not speak French. Sandburg is then supposed to have gone into a rage, saying in effect, that all that about Paris being the poetic center was hokum, that Chicago could just as well be the center, and that they would make it so, etc., etc. America was as good as France, better because less exhausted, it had native inspiration, etc., lacked all that corruption, etc. Now after forty years, how has the story ended? Yeats is considered the greatest poet of the century in the English language, and Sandburg is in Arkansas with his goats and his guitar. These stories are not stories so much as myths, that happen over and over again.

The danger, it seems to me, of Mr. Creeley's group, and the San Francisco group, is that they will go the way of Sandburg. In fact, there is a strange resemblance between the Chicago group of the 1910's and the San Francisco group of the 1950's. In forty years, the city has shifted 1,500 miles farther west, but there is still the moving attempt to raise up a culture in an isolated city by any means possible; in both movements there is the thought that poetry can only be written by the uncorrupted and innocent; an emphasis on street poetry and prostitutes; and an emphasis on the strictly 'Amurrican', as Pound would say. One senses that the majority of the San Francisco group, with the exception of Mr. Rexroth, is all too ready to describe French poetry as 'Rimbaud and all that'; we remember that Charles Olson, in Mr. Creeley's group, is an authority not on some foreign poet, but on the American, Melville; and that all the doctrines of the man they perhaps respect the most, Williams, emphasize the Americanism of material, words, meters, and attitude as subjects for poetry.

These thoughts about isolationism from the newer poetry of Europe are never too distant as we consider Robert Creeley's poems themselves. Robert Creeley has a lovely poem to William Carlos Williams, in which he is thinking perhaps of the troubles in Williams' life:

> The pleasure of the wit sustains
> a vague aroma
>
> The fox glove (unseen) the
> wild flower
>
> To the hands come
> many things. In time of trouble
>
> a wild exultation.

What is the weakness in this poem? Obviously it is lack of images, just as the same thing is the weakness of Williams' poetry itself. The language suffers a kind of drought from lack of images. Yet the use of images is particularly the tradition of modern poetry which comes to us from abroad.

Perhaps we can see the incompatibility of abstract words and images better in another poem. Mr. Creeley opens:

By Saturday I said you would be better on Sunday.
The insistence was a part of a reconciliation.

It is strange to see this. It seems to me that the greatest tradition of all modern poetry, and of the *avant-garde* for a century has been the heavy use of images. Poems are imagined in which everything is said by image, and nothing by direct statement at all. The poem *is* the images, images touching all the senses, uniting the world beneath and the world above, as in Lorca's:

> Black horses pass
> And dark people
> Over the deep roads
> Of the guitar.

These wild images we first notice in French poetry of the 19th century, in Baudelaire for instance. There is a great blossoming in Mallarmé and Rimbaud, and in this century, it is made into a whole way of thought by the poets in the Spanish language. In French, also, images continue to be the strength of modern poetry, both in the Surrealists and in such poets as Eluard and Char. But in this poetry, or in America itself, this tradition does not exist.

There are other great traditions in modern poetry; a second great direction is that of going deeply into oneself, and returning like an explorer, perhaps saddened forever, but with strange kinds of knowledge—the tradition, for instance, of Rilke and Trakl. Yet, to anyone who knows this work it is apparent that the poetry of which we are speaking does not share this tradition—the connection with the world is never broken.

A third great movement of modern poetry, and an invention horrifying to the bourgeois, is the simple description of life in modern cities, life after the Industrial Revolution, life exactly as it is, of which the first poems were written by Baudelaire, as, for instance, in his *Dusk Before Dawn:*

Houses, here and there, commence to give off smoke.
Women of happiness, with eyelids the color of ashes,
Mouths fallen open, sleep the sleep of beasts.
And women without a cent, dragging their thin and cold breasts,
Blow on their coals, and blow on their hands.
It was the time of night, when, among cold and pinching of pennies,
The pains increase of the women in labour;
Like a sob that is cut by a jet of blood
The cry of a cock far off slashed the smoky air,
A sea of fog bathed the monumental buildings. . . .

Like a face in tears which the gusts try to dry
The air is full of the whispering sounds of things that at last escape,
And man is sick of writing, and woman of making love.

Eliot in 1915 wrote:

> They are rattling breakfast plates in basement kitchens,
> And along the trampled edges of the street
> I am aware of the damp souls of housemaids
> Sprouting despondently at area gates.

To those who know Mr. Creeley's work, it is obvious that there is nothing of this sort here either: the poems like those of Pound, after he left London, exist in some indeterminate place which is never described. Some of Eliot's descriptions of cities, though written forty years ago, are still the best in the English language; in German, there are poems by Rilke and Gottfried Benn, but none in America at all.

A fourth of the great traditions of modern poetry is a kind of daring in self-revelation—one thinks immediately of La Forgue's wild descriptions of himself as a clown, an orphan, a weathercock, a worshipper of the moon, a terrified admirer of women, a hunting horn, an eternal failure. This daring seems to start with Gautier. Baudelaire is nourished by it, and it occupies nearly the entire work of Corbière. But in the poetry of which we are speaking the poet clings to his own personality too tightly, as if he might lose it, and nothing can be achieved here. It comes as a start then to realize that this poetry, though presented in this country as *avant-garde*, does not share at all in four of the greatest traditions of modern literature or *avant-garde* poetry. This is true both of the San Francisco group and the Black Mountain group, as well as of Mr. Creeley's poetry itself.

Well, what is modern about it then? For it is obvious that Creeley's poems are modern, just as it is obvious, for instance, that William Meredith's poems are not. Let us compare a stanza of Mr. Meredith's with one of Mr. Creeley's. Mr. Meredith opens a poem:

> What will I ask, if one free wish comes down
> Along with all these prodigalities
> That we pick up like dollars in a dream,
> And what I urge you ask, is not that we
> Grow single in our passion without gap,
> Losing with loneliness dear differences;
> Nor lust, to burn a lifetime resinously,
> Although that surely were a miracle....
>
> from *A Boon*, by William Meredith,
> from *New Poets of England and America*.

Robert Creeley writes of his children:

> Where fire is, they are quieter
> and sit, comforted. They were born
> by their mother in hopelessness.
>
> But in them I had been, at first,
> tongue. If they speak,
> I have myself and love them.

The first thing one asks, when one finishes the Meredith stanza, is, what kind of a man is it, that, speaking to his own wife or girl, would ever say:

> Grow single in our passion without gap,
> Losing with loneliness dear differences;

It is impossible. No one would speak like that. In Elizabethan times, and in another country, they actually spoke like that but that was three hundred years ago. Mr. Meredith writes of his emotions as if he were living in Elizabethan times, and the whole thing comes through to us, as it cannot help but do, with an air of phoniness.

When Mr. Creeley, speaking of the strange sense of self-possession one's own children give to a parent, says:

> If they speak,
> I have myself, and love them

it strikes us that people today speak with that voice. In syntax, in diction, in every way, tone, attitude toward love, these two poems about love are in total contrast. The greatest difference perhaps is in the words: in Mr. Creeley's poem, the words are honest and convincing—a quality which Mr. Creeley learned from William Carlos Williams, or perhaps, learned by himself, I don't know. One of the greatest of modern traditions is the use of our own words, of modern words. Somehow we are very reluctant to do this. We find it hard to admit the world has changed as much as it has, and we want to hedge our bets, so to speak, and use words the immortals used. Mr. Creeley has not done this. His poems exist in the modern vocabulary, or not at all, and his poems have been from the start sharp and without the apology of rhyme. As a result, he is very much at home in this language, and at times so much at home, that he plays, and decides to go farther out into slang:

> As I sd to my
> friend, because I am
> always talking,—John, I
>
> sd, which was not his
> name, the darkness sur-
> rounds us, what
>
> can we do against
> it, or else, shall we &
> why not, but a goddamn big car,

> drive, he sd, for
> christ's sake, look
> out where yr going.

I think this is a fine poem, and that it makes most other poems in slang look silly. It succeeds in exactly the points where they fail, namely in a kind of sensitivity and resonance. In the use of this kind of language, which in one sense is the only language we have, almost all American poets are behind Mr. Creeley. This is one part of modern poetry in which his work does share.

The relationship between men and women as subject matter for poetry is another great modern tradition. It is hard for us to realize that through the 19th century of Wordsworth, Keats, Shelley, Tennyson, Hopkins, Bridges, etc., this poetry virtually dropped out of existence. The poems were not about the relationship between men and women, but Grecian urns, Chapman's Homer, Intellectual Beauty, the Lake Country, King Arthur's court, autumn, etc., and if women are discussed, it is in a dreamy 'poetic' way. Suddenly real women have returned, at first in Baudelaire, and then strongly in La Forgue, in his case almost his entire subject matter, and in Eliot, in Eluard, in the magnificent poems of Neruda. In America this tradition has been represented by Eliot in his youth, and through his entire life by William Carlos Williams.

One of the most interesting qualities of Robert Creeley's work, as it is of Louis Simpson's, is the presence of women.

As he says in *The Warning*:

> For love—I would
> split open your head and put
> a candle in
> behind the eyes.

Let us choose a poem in which the two traditions present in Robert Creeley coincide—the use of modern words and the presence of women. We find in him a man who will use modern words in a poem at any risk, even the risk of bad taste or being temporarily the tough guy, and a man who is evidently kind and gentle, and who loves and respects women:

>   Nothing for a dirty man
>   but soap in his bathtub, a
>
>   greasy hand, lover's
>   nuts
>   perhaps. Or else
>
>   something like sand
>   with which to scour him
>
>   for all
>   that is lovely in women.

In *The Carnival*, writing perhaps of love, he says:

>   Whereas the man who hits
>   the gong dis-
>   proves it, in all its
>   simplicity—
>   Even so the attempt
>   makes for triumph, in
>   another man.
>
>   Likewise in love I
>   am not foolish or in-
>   competent. My method is not a
>
>   tenderness, but hope
>   defined.

A last invention of modern poetry I will mention here is poetry about the increasingly invisible, but increasingly apparent, oppression in all countries. Garcia Lorca wrote some of the first of this poetry, and was shot by Franco. This element of his poetry is as important I think as the folk element, for which he is so much praised. When Lorca writes of the Spanish State Police:

>   Their horses are black.
>   The hoofs of their horses are black.

And:
>With a patent leather soul,
>They come riding down the road,
>Hunched over and living at night,
>Wherever they go, they cause
>Silences made of black rubber,
>And fears of fine sand.
>They go by, if they wish to,
>And in their heads they hold
>A vague astronomy
>Of heavenly pistols.

When Lorca writes so, he is writing a poetry of which, either in images or subject matter, we know very little in this country. This tradition does not exist in William Carlos Williams, nor, except in a sort of cloudy way, in Pound, and not at all in Mr. Eliot, who, in any event, is so much on the side of authority that he is obliged to forgive much of what they do. Lorca is quite a different man. The events in his *Gypsy Ballads* are a symbol of the increasing defeats of the poor in their battle with the rich. It is interesting to see this sense of oppression suddenly appear in Mr. Creeley's work, with a touch of bitter humor. He has a poem called *After Lorca*, which I will quote entire:

>The church is a business, and the rich
>are the business men.
>   When they pull on the bells, the
>poor come piling in and when a poor man dies, he has a
>   wooden
>cross, and they rush through the ceremony.
>
>But when a rich man dies, they
>drag out the Sacrament
>and a golden Cross, and go doucement, doucement
>to the cemetery.
>
>And the poor love it
>and think it's crazy.

This is a good poem too. We notice again the tremendous power of contemporary words, when someone who understands them uses them. In this poem, once more, the language often becomes slang, as in the last word, upon which the whole poem depends. If the poem is sometimes weak, as it is, it is not because of the contemporary words, but because the poem is not contemporary enough; the language is treated in too flat, or English, a way—unlike Lorca, himself, whose wild attitude and wild, deep treatment of the language make a strange unity.

This must be the end of a short tour through Mr. Creeley's work. His poems give the sense of a man who has considerable integrity and is difficult and stubborn. Though the resemblances to old men such as Williams and Pound are too clear to be mistaken, nevertheless there is a distinct originality, for when we read his poems, we are led toward quite different thoughts; the reverberations in our mind, so to speak, are different, and certainly richer, than those from the rather barren work of such earlier men as Larsson or Lowenfels. Still we feel a shock to realize that this poetry, which is thought of in this country as *avant-garde*, and perhaps is the most *avant-garde* we have, is really not *avant-garde* at all. The poems seem quite isolated from the great richness and daring of Spanish poetry, or French poetry, and somewhat also from their delicate sensibility and joy, as well as their savagery. Mr. Creeley has great sensitivity to the American language, and great honesty, but it seems at the service of a too narrow and barren tradition. These poems, and those of the entire Black Mountain and San Francisco groups, are based almost entirely, it seems to me, on the American tradition. The American tradition is not rich enough; it is short, Puritanical, and has only one or two first-rate poets in it, and the faults of the lesser poets are always the same—a kind of barrenness and abstraction. I think Mr. Creeley should try to deepen his own imagination, perhaps by learning a new poetry in another language, certainly by searching for more richness of language and image. Mr. Creeley is still very young, and his poems, even so far, are a contribution to American literature, but I think his work also shows that sheer honesty and the American literary tradition alone are not enough to make a rich *avant-garde*.
—Crunk

A NOTE ON SYLLABICS

SOME POETS MAY CONTINUE TO WRITE in iambs, some in no meter at all, some may invent a meter of their own, others find an interest in a meter such as syllabics.

I. In syllabics, the only unit of measure is the number of syllables in the line. It takes no account of stress or length at all. Consequently, with the power moving freely about the line, extremely original and powerful rhythms may be set up. Poems in syllabics have been written by Marianne Moore, and others, and several poets of the fifties have begun to experiment with the meter. Syllabics are and always have been used in French and Italian.

II. Some of the possibilities for a whole poem might be: a whole poem of nine-syllable lines, for instance, or eleven-syllable lines. The first stanza of the poem 'England: the Nation in the Sea' in the first issue of *The Fifties* is written, for instance, in lines of six syllables:

> Cold air of the heath, black
> Air of black dukes of death

It is possible to have a close alternation of lines of different lengths; for instance, alternately nine and eleven syllables. 'Marat's Death', for instance, in the first issue, is written in two seven-syllable lines followed by an eight-syllable line.

One might also have a more elaborate organization. Marianne Moore's poem, 'What are Years', or her magnificent poem, 'In Distrust of Merits' are written in the more elaborate form: many lines, all of different lengths, but the stanza repeated exactly.

Syllabics may be rhymed or not rhymed. The off-sound rhyme, duty/sea; sent/parent; hunted/dead, continues the muting of distinctions of volume; it is firmly anti-iambic. Odd numbers of syllables seem to work best for somewhat the same reason—they help to avoid the insidious iambic. If you use this meter, be particularly careful to avoid the possibility of an iambic reading at the beginning of the poem. The poet must establish firmly the anti-iambic convention from the start. It is best to avoid the alternation of speech stresses which forces an iambic pattern on anyone used to English verse.

III. To avoid the iambic meter is to avoid not only its many uses but its many associations. The associations may be personal. I find it difficult, for instance, to avoid false feeling in iambics, and here also, syllabics have allowed me, by the new areas of feeling which it has made possible, to discover new poems. Syllabics give the English language a new sound, allow a more intimate tone, and possess the authority (as well as the motives and feelings) of direct, plain speech. Of course you have to play it by ear. If it feels like measure to the poet, it is measure enough. Iambics increasingly seem to assume a form of artificiality which demands a huge rhetoric for success, like the Robert Lowell of *Lord Weary's Castle*. Most younger poets are unable to achieve the rhetoric, and as a result they fake, and I believe the phony gorgeosity of much contemporary diction has a metrical source. The other direction from rhetoric is plain speech, and plain speech is the force of the syllabic meter.

There are other variations in this very free and open meter: the stanza with an unchanging number of syllables, for instance, may be apportioned into lines of differing lengths from stanza to stanza, or even into differing numbers of lines, but this has not been tried much, and I don't know how successful it would be. But for me, syllabics are so far the only point at which the possibilities of speech coincide with the mysterious arbitrariness of poetic form.

—Abednego

JUAN RAMÓN JIMÉNEZ

I

¡Intelijencia, dame
el nombre exacto de las cosas!
.·. . Que mi palabra sea
la cosa misma,
creada por mi alma nuevamente.
Que por mí vayan todos
los que no las conocen, a las cosas;
que por mí vayan todos
los que ya las olvidan, a las cosas;
que por mí vayan todos
los mismos que las aman, a las cosas . . .
¡Intelijencia, dame
el nombre exacto, y tuyo,
y suyo, y mío, de las cosas!

Juan Ramón Jiménez

I

Intelligence, give me
The exact name of things!
. . . Let my word be
The thing itself,
Created by my soul anew.
Let all who do not know them
Go to the things, through me;
Let all who now forget them
Go to the things, through me;
Let all the ones who love them
Go to the things, through me . . .
Intelligence, give me
The name exact, and thine,
And theirs, and mine, of things!

2

Tarde última y serena,
corta como una vida,
fin de todo lo amado;
¡yo quiero ser eterno!

—Atravesando hojas,
el sol, ya cobre, viene
a herirme el corazón.
¡Yo quiero ser eterno!—

Belleza que yo he visto,
¡no te borres ya nunca!
Por que seas eterna,
¡yo quiero ser eterno!

3

Ocaso

¡Oh, qué sonido de oro que se va,
de oro que ya se va a la eternidad;
qué triste nuestro oído, de escuchar
ese oro que se va a la eternidad,
este silencio que se va a quedar
sin su oro que se va a la eternidad!

2

Serene last evening,
Short as a life,
End of all that was loved;
I want to be eternal!

—Traversing leaves,
The sun, already copper, comes
To wound my heart.
I want to be eternal!—

Beauty that I have seen,
Don't ever fade away!
So that you be eternal,
I want to be eternal!

3

Sunset

Oh, what a sound of gold that leaves,
Of gold that leaves already for eternity;
How sad our ear, from listening to
That gold that's leaving for eternity,
This silence which is to be left
Without its gold that's leaving for eternity!

4

Ruta

Todos duermen, abajo.
                Arriba, alertas,
el timonel y yo.

El, mirando la aguja, dueño de
los cuerpos, con sus llaves
echadas. Yo, los ojos
en lo infinito, guiando
los tesoros abiertos de las almas.

5

Yo no soy yo.
                    Soy este
que va a mi lado sin yo verlo;
que, a veces, voy a ver,
y que, a veces, olvido.
El que calla, sereno, cuando hablo,
el que perdona, dulce, cuando odio,
el que pasea por donde no estoy,
el que quedará en pie cuando yo muera.

4

Route

All are asleep, below.
                         Above, alert,
The helmsman and I.

   He, looking at the compass, owner of
The bodies, with the locks
Fastened. I, with my eyes
In the infinite, guiding
The open treasures of the souls.

5

   I am not I.
                         I am this one
Who goes by my side unseen by me;
Whom I, at times, go visit,
And whom I, at times, forget.
He who keeps silent, serene, when I speak,
He who forgives, sweet, when I hate,
He who takes a walk where I am not,
He who will remain standing when I die.

6

Fué lo mismo
que un crepúsculo inmenso de oro alegre,
que, de repente, se apagara todo,
en un nublado de ceniza.

—Me dejó esa tristeza
de los afanes grandes, cuando tienen
que encerrarse en la jaula
de la verdad diaria; ese pesar
de los jardines de colores ideales,
que borra una luz sucia de petróleo—.

Yo no me resignaba.
Le lloré; le obligué. Vi la ridícula
sinrazón de esta cándida hermandad
de hombre y vida,
de muerte y hombre.

¡Y aquí estoy, vivo ridículo, esperando,
muerto ridículo, a la muerte!

6

It was the same
As an immense sunset of joyful gold,
Which, suddenly, should be wholly extinguished,
In a cloud of ashes.

—He left me that sadness
Of the great aspirations, when they must
Lock themselves in the cage
Of daily truth; that sorrow
Of the gardens of ideal colours,
Which a dirty light of oil effaces—.

I could not resign myself.
I grieved over him; I obliged him. I saw the ridiculous
Injustice of this candid brotherhood
Of man and life,
Of death and man.

And here I am, ridiculous living man, waiting,
Ridiculous dead man, for death!

7

Cenit

Yo no seré yo, muerte,
hasta que tú te unas con mi vida
y me completes así todo;
hasta que mi mitad de luz se cierre
con mi mitad de sombra
—y sea yo equilibrio eterno
en la mente del mundo:
unas veces, mi medio yo, radiante;
otras, mi otro medio yo, en olvido.—

Yo no seré yo, muerte,
hasta que tú, en tu turno, vistas
de huesos pálidos mi alma.

7

Zenith

I shall not be I, death,
Until thou shalt unite with my life
And thus complete me all;
Until my half of light shall close
With my half of shadow
—And I shall be eternal equilibrium
In the mind of the world:
Sometimes, my half I, radiant;
Sometimes, my other half I, in oblivion.—

I shall not be I, death,
Until thou, in thy turn, shalt dress
My soul with pale bones.

> *All poems are from Jiménez:*
> Tercera antolojía poética (*Madrid,
> Editorial Biblioteca Nueva,* 1957) *and*
> Libros de poesía (*Madrid, Aguilar,* 1957),
> *translated by Carlos de Francisco Zea.*

REPLY TO CECIL HEMLEY

IN *New World Writing* #11, Mr. Hemley says that art has reached its limits. Evidently all artists agree, since no opposition has been made in the two years since. He writes: 'By the 1930's, the new subject matter had been explored, the old cosmos had been destroyed, and the limits of art reached.' Yet it is apparent that the subject matter of today has hardly been touched, because, like the tide, it is continually coming up, or like experience itself, it is continually being created. Consider, for instance, some of the historical events since the 1920's and the more subtle transformations that have followed them. Concentration camps affected millions directly and their very existence stunned the world. This terror is somehow connected with the indifference of people in suburbs. The general apathy, apathy toward ideals, apathy toward suffering, is now an accepted part of suburban living. This indifference is also a sort of cocoon comfort of which the people of the 1910's and '20's knew nothing. The dominance of the West, the habit people in the West have of forgetting all other people, is obviously ending. In America, again, an IBM plant comes in; switch shifts do not provide for eight-day novenas—or family life. The Industrial Revolution has affected life more in the last thirty years than in the one hundred years before. It is unbelievable that the subject matter of the Industrial Revolution should have been exhausted in the 1915-1930 period.

After saying that the 'new subject matter' has been totally explored, Mr. Hemley says, 'To the rear, march', that 'This is the predicament of modern art; there is no place to go but backward'. Art is not like a commuter train on a one-trunk line that goes only to one place and backs up at night. Art may go in whatever direction it chooses. It is not bound by a mechanical tradition or by a literary leader at the throttle. Art is more natural, more able, like a bird choosing its own course. The future does not lie in returning to the old and reactionary. It lies in recognizing, using, and forming the powerful present into a new kind of art. More is at stake here than flimsy experimentation.

In many ways, Cecil Hemley is like an old crippled uncle at Kitty Hawk, who says to the Wright brothers: 'It won't fly!' 'You've been trying long enough.' Then he turns to the crowd and says, 'They'll all kill themselves'. This defeatism, this kill-joy quality, leads Mr. Hemley, playing the part of the old man on the lonely field after the plane has flown, to warn all the young men standing around, 'Maybe it worked today, but it won't work tomorrow!'

Sadly, Mr. Hemley argues, 'But as I have said, the modern movement no longer appears capable of producing significant work.' If this is true, how are we to explain the work of Gottfried Benn in this issue? These poems are the poems of a man who has swum in all the currents of modern life, and in the sensitive artistry of the modern movement, and at the end of his life produces new work. Benn's thoughts on this problem are interesting, too. In his late *Problems of Lyric Poetry*, written in 1951, which is translated in the Autumn 1958 *Western Review*, he writes:

> I will know that even amid the ranks of modern lyric poets, voices are heard that call for a turning back. It is Eliot, who in an essay in the *Merkur*, is of the opinion that this tendency must come to a stop, i.e. the progression of self-consciousness, this extreme emphasis upon semantics and language as such and the pains taken to surpass the boundaries of it—but Eliot also fights against television and would obstruct it. I believe that he is wrong in both cases; I believe that he is basicly mistaken. I am of the opinion that the phenomena of which we are speaking are irreversible and announce rather the beginning than the end of a development. . . .

The poems of Benn printed here give something new, not only to his own work, but to the vigorous modern movement itself. And the movement is not only the work of old men. The work considered the best in the German language after the War is the poetry of the young Austrian surrealist poet, Paul Celan.

—WILLIAM DUFFY

THE POSSIBILITY OF NEW POETRY

For some time it has been evident that the iambic style is becoming more and more ineffective. This old style, with the iamb, its caesuras, its rhymes, its thousands of rhythms reminding us of other poems and other countries, its delicate ways, by slight shifts, of indicating slight shifts of feelings, its elegant stanzas, its old tested devices of pauses and counterpauses, is like a man speaking who gestures too much. The audience, as it watches, sees every minute too many gestures, and finally becomes lost, unable to relate the gestures to the emotion being expressed or the subject, and finally, in despair, must ignore the gestures entirely, and simply listen to the flow of words—and now *many more words are needed*. But in the new poetry, the contrary is true—there is no necessity in the form itself for continual gesture, by rhyme, etc.—therefore, if you raise your little finger once, slowly, it has tremendous meaning.

★ ★ ★ ★ ★ ★ ★ ★ ★ ★ ★

The old English style depended somehow on repetition. A sonnet, for instance, takes one idea, and then repeats it in slightly different form in the next two stanzas, and this kind of repetition is the essence of a Shakespearean sonnet—it is *its kind of concentration*—a concentration on one idea through three stanzas—but this kind of repetition, as it has come down through the 18th and 19th centuries, etc., tends to explain the emotion, not express it. Consequently, in the poetry today we have thousands of ideas vaguely connected with emotions, but no emotion at all.

A PARAGRAPH OF VALÉRY

ANYONE WHO LOOKS at the recent book, *The Art of Poetry,* Valéry's essays on poetry which Jackson Mathews edited for Bollingen, will see that Valéry is obviously not the flinty supporter of classical form at all costs, as he is usually presented. His mind is joyful, adventurous, sarcastic, and he is, unlike our classical critics, full of admiration for the more advanced work. In this interesting passage, sent to us by James Wright, he suggested that it is not as the bourgeois world would have it, namely, that we understand and love radical work in our youth, and as we grow more mature, understand classical work, but the other way around.

> The same man may change his tastes and his style, burn at twenty what he adored at sixteen; *some kind of inner transmutation* shifts the power of seduction from one master to another. The lover of Musset becomes more *mature* and leaves him for Verlaine. Another, after being first nourished by Hugo, devotes himself completely to Mallarmé.
> These spiritual changes generally operate in one particular *direction* rather than in the other, which is much less probable: it must be extremely rare for *Le Bateau Ivre* to lead eventually to *Le Lac*. On the other hand, by loving the pure and hard *Herodiade*, one does not lose one's taste for the *Prière d'Esther*. These defections, these sudden accesses of love or of grace, these conversions and substitutions, this possibility of being successively *sensitized* to the work of incompatible poets, are literary phenomena of the first importance. Therefore no one ever mentions them.
>
> *From* Problems of Poetry (1936) *by Paul Valéry, translated by Denise Folliot.*

JAMES WRIGHT

IN THE HARD SUN

> *Dark cypresses—*
> *The world is uneasily happy;*
> *It will all be forgotten.*
> —*Storm.*

Mother of roots, you have not seeded
The tall ashes of loneliness
For me.
One loop of tendril bound me long ago.
Therefore, proud mother, cedarn, oaken, firred
With scarped crowns, and the last the laurel of seas
Where the butterflies of garbage scows
Rise and blossom,
Now I go.

If I knew the name,
Your name, all trellises of vineyards and old fire
Would quicken to shake terribly my
Earth, mother of spiralling searches (tall, bell tooth,
        terrible
Fable of calcium, and girl). I crept this afternoon
In weeds once more,
Casual, daydreaming you might not strike
Me down. Mother of window sills and journeys,
Hallower of scratching hands,
The sight of my blind man makes me want to weep.
Tiller of waves or whatever, woman or man,
Mother of roots or father of diamonds,
Look: I am nothing.
I do not even have ashes to rub into my eyes.

IN FEAR OF HARVESTS

It has happened
Before: nearby,
The nostrils of slow horses
Breathe evenly,
And the brown bees drag their high garlands
Heavily,
Toward hives of snow.

Robert Bly

THE ARMY OF ADVERTISING MEN

The merchants of death come
Swimming through the air
On mahogany boxes and leaves of China tea.
They come in ornate galleons of false pity
Or on the red wagon of a child
Through the solid and sordid rain.

Beneath their eyelids they carry the crystal spear
Of the Conquistador,
The burning tear of the unwanted child,
And the sleepy oils of the Inquisitor.

They have vowed to fight for Morgan,
And in their eyes there is a promise
To leave
The ground behind them smoking.

POEM IN THREE PARTS

I.

Oh, on an early morning I think I shall live forever!
I am wrapped in my joyful flesh,
As the grass is wrapt in its clouds of green.

II.

Rising from a bed, where I dreamt
Of long rides past castles and hot coals,
The sun lies happily on my knees;
I have suffered and survived the night
Bathed in dark water, like any blade of grass.

III.

The strong leaves of the box elder tree,
Plunging in the wind, call us to disappear
Into the wilds of the universe,
Where we shall sit at the foot of a plant,
And live forever, like the dust.

Thomas Parnell

LA DAME FRANCE—1958

Lost echoes, the black
And ominous sights it
Sucked from sandy
Thirsty Algiers.

Its dark flowing figures, cold,
Chilled by desert nights,
Brandished in the sun,
Tribal dancers chanting.

But 'la belle dame
Sans merci' gathers her frightened warriors,
Her old napoleonic generals,
And commands a halt.

THE BATAAN DEATH MARCH

Under the rusty can in the roadside ditch,
                                      it's there.

Under the hood of the '49 Ford,
                                it's there.

In contract homes on bareback streets,
                              you find it.

Hidden in piles of U.S. corn,
        Or in the files of General Motors.

SOME NEW BOOKS

S. F. VANNI, the Italian bookseller at 30 West 12th Street, New York, has published a fine book called *The Promised Land*, consisting of poems by the four great Italian poets of this century, Umberto Saba, Giuseppe Ungaretti, Eugenio Montale, and Salvatore Quasimodo, with an introduction by Prof. Pacifici. The translations, by several hands, vary in quality, but the Italian is included facing all poems. It is available from Mr. Vanni for $1.50. It is highly recommended.

★ ★ ★ ★ ★ ★ ★ ★ ★ ★ ★

Jerome Rothenberg is publishing a series of young poets in his Hawk's Well Press. The first of these is by Seymour Faust, and has a fantastic introduction by Faust himself, and the second is by Thom Gunn. He is also planning a book of poems by Ralph Pomeroy, and has already published some prose by Martin Buber and Matsuo Basho.

Mr. Rothenberg is without a question one of the best translators of German in this country; and we have some of his translations of the young Austrian surrealist poet, Paul Celan, in the next issue of this magazine. These poems of Celan, with others, will also appear in the anthology *New Young German Poets*, which Mr. Rothenberg is preparing for Ferlingetti at City Lights for spring publication. Hawk's Well Press books may be obtained at bookstores, or from Mr. Rothenberg, for about a dollar, at 600 W. 163rd Street, New York.

★ ★ ★ ★ ★ ★ ★ ★ ★ ★ ★

Gaetano Massa, who owns and runs the Las Americas Publishing House and bookstore at 249 West 13th Street, New York, has for a long time published a series of small books of Puerto Rican poets, and of Puerto Rican poets living in the United States. He is now beginning a series of bi-lingual books, both Spanish and English, of which the first will be W. S. Merwin's translation of *The Cid*, and a collection of poems by the Spanish poet Antonio Machado, translated by Willis Barnstone. These books will sell for about a dollar, and are available from Mr. Massa at 249 West 13th Street.

ON ENGLISH AND AMERICAN POETRY

MANY OF THE POEMS which I see suffer from a single fault, that of extremely abstract language. One sees many lines such as:

    Aiming at the hydrofaction of tranquillity

or

                    This is a public place
    Achieved against subjective odds.

or

    And times are hastening, yet disguise is mortal

or

    Here in the present tense, disguise is mortal

Actually the last three lines are from a poem by W. S. Graham in a fine magazine, the October 1958 *Poetry*. It indicates the possibility, which is also my own belief, that this tendency to abstract language comes to us primarily from Great Britain. The Scottish poets merely suffer from a trouble more violent in England.

Strangely enough, it is not the Germans nor the Spanish nor the French who have introduced abstraction into poetry, but the English. Possibly this is not so surprising. England has always been proud of her subjection of the emotions to the intellect, or to put it another way, her control of the dark passions. She is proud of her ability to go on quietly with plans for Empire despite the suffering of the dark natives on whom she imposes, as in the subjection of India in the 19th century or the Mau-Mau rebellion of the 20th. The intellect looks on everything abstractly; that is its efficiency. Long ago, England evidently decided to prefer intellect and will to emotion, and she enforced it in the Public Schools. As they say: 'The Empire was won on the playing fields of Eton'. She has continued until at last even the poets were affected.

For whatever reason, the poetry of England has become increasingly abstract and intellectual in the last hundred years. From Keats to Tennyson to Auden to Graham to Tomlinson the movement is unmistakable. Yet this intellectualism and abstraction are so fatal to poetry that the English poets of this generation seem the poorest of the sixty-five generations of English poets since Chaucer's time. Yet the motion has such impetus that these younger poets have been forced to raise this destructive abstraction to a virtue and to develop theories that enthusiasm and passions are vulgar, etc. A reader of René Char or Lorca finds this a pitiful scene to watch. The poets are not to be blamed—they can write nothing else, and perhaps no poet could in their situation.

Although American and English poetry have been taking increasingly divergent courses, one thing should be noticed. During the period when American poetry was growing, and in her spring, namely in the late 19th and the early 20th centuries, another poetry in the same language was in the process of dying. That was a coincidence that has rarely happened before; usually a poetry and a language grow together. In this case, American poetry was growing and English poetry was in a process of gradual sterility and petrifaction. The effect of English poetry of the last hundred years on American poetry has been disastrous.

For every poet, such as Whitman, who breaks free of its influence, a thousand succumb and are destroyed. It is no accident that the three most daring and massive poets in the American language in the twentieth century—Wallace Stevens, T. S. Eliot, and Ezra Pound—have all immersed themselves in French, not English. Wallace Stevens, as he says, learned his sensibility from the French, and is called sometimes the only French poet in the language; Eliot wrote in French, and his work has been called 'the best translation of La Forgue that will ever be done'; and Pound spent years translating Provencal poetry, not to mention Chinese. Since then not only has the French tradition deepened, but there are traditions possibly greater than the French.

But we still have not broken free of the English. Many of the poems in the quarterlies of the West are a blizzard of abstract words—no different in that respect from those in the *Kenyon Review*. On the one hand, poets in the universities try to write about American experiences using English stanza forms, while others on the loose in Los Angeles or San Francisco reject the stanza forms and meter only to adopt wholesale the English habit of barren excitement and abstract words. Both are as far from the modern tradition of the deep images of the unconscious as possible. If they study a French poet in California it is usually Prévert, who of all French poets is the nearest the English; they are as far from the French tradition of Rimbaud and Eluard as could be imagined, which is also a tradition of the deep images of the unconscious.

Let us leave the English tradition alone. Its poets must become more and more abstract, as the birds of indifference and empire come home to roost, but in America we are just beginning; we are hardly in our third or fourth generation of poets. If we have vigorous teachers we can write strong, vigorous poetry, but those teachers, those poets, write, as they always do, in other languages—not in our own. They write in the Spanish tradition, suddenly reborn in the last fifty years, or in the French tradition through Char, in which so much sensibility is nourished, or in the German tradition of Rilke and Trakl, poetry which is not dying, but growing —poetry which has found a way to include not only more of the mood of modern life than any before, but also more of the joy of the unconscious.

—Robert Bly.

Madame Tussaud's Wax Museum

PERHAPS THE DEADEST POEMS being written today are those with 'classical references'. In our opinion, this is not an isolated quirk, but part of a general attempt to make a dead language more interesting. However, since Zeus, or Troy, or Aeneas have no emotional meaning for us at all, these words act as a sort of open sluice to drain all the sincerity and emotion out of a poem in which they appear. Consequently, the usual effect of a classical reference is to kill the poem instantly. It seemed, therefore, as editors, that we should warn the very young poets against imitating poems such as these:

from AMPHIMACHOS THE DANDY

Amphimachos, old Homer's fool,
strolled into battle girt in gold
A dandy of the Karian school,
he had a pool of bold
coruscation amidst the bronze,
as who should say: 'For me the day
'is enough. Let the cold wands
'of the enemy strike. I act the play—
—*Vincent McHugh*

from THE GREATER MUSIC

But only Orpheus,
when the fierce hand plucked his strings,
could not consent to the divisions

of the lute. His breath, greeting
the stone-deaf, eager stones (though why
those fury-flying stones did not hear
and build into a tower of hearing

around his air I cannot tell)
—*T. Weiss*

from IULUS

Never had child a more adventurous life
Than young Iulus, fled from vanquished Troy's
Burnt palaces, her ruined shores, the noise
Of Greek and Trojan, loud in barbarous strife.
—*Eleanor Glenn Wallis*

from ORACLE AT DELPHI

King Croesus carried to Apollo's sibyl
    Gifts golden to the core,
Infallible gold shining as her syllables
    Shone: Croesus was fully aware
Truth came highly priced and hard, like war.
—*Robert Bagg*

TOURIST

I passed Olympus in the night,
But had I passed by day,
I still could tell you less of it
Than blind Homer may.
—*Mark Van Doren*

All poems here are from New Poems by American Poets #2 *(Ballantine, 1957), edited by Rolfe Humphries.*

Suggested resolutions for young poets:

I. I promise I will neither write nor read another poem on the death of Orpheus as long as I live.

II. I promise I will never describe the sad fate of Oedipus in a poem again, on pain of losing my eyes.

III. I promise I will never capture poor Perseus and drag him into my poems, nor Aeneas, nor good Achilles, nor Telamon, nor Penelope, mainly because no one knows who Perseus is.

WISDOM OF THE OLD

WE HAVE GRAVE DOUBTS ABOUT THE intelligence of most, if not all, the older men in the country, as our note on Ray West in the last issue perhaps indicated. Another, I suppose, is Leslie Fiedler. He hates men without large families, and we know what he thinks of Huck Finn and Tom Sawyer, Hemingway, etc.: everywhere he looks he sees homosexuality. One of our readers recently wrote us: 'I enjoyed your Wisdom of the Old in the last issue, and the thought struck me: What would happen if Fiedler were given Churchill's *History of the English-Speaking Peoples* to review?'

THE HISTORY OF THE ENGLISH-SPEAKING PEOPLES

a review by

LESLIE WIEDLER

Out here in Montana, we often read Churchill's *History of the English-Speaking Peoples* and I think because of the many cows out here, we have more insight into the book than those in the East. I wonder how many have noticed, for instance, that most of the characters in Churchill's book are men? For example, Richard II, Richard III, King Henry V, etc.—almost all the kings he describes are men! Moreover, he often describes large groups of men going out in the field with guns—that is his favorite subject, in fact—sometimes two or three thousand of them. *Why don't they take their wives with them?* I think the conclusion is obvious, and we know that Churchill's mother was born in America.

AWARD

THE ORDER OF THE BLUE TOAD is herewith awarded to Gilbert Highet for continual degradation of the literature of Greece and Rome. He finds all literature best if easily understood and a little jolly. He carries on the incessant academic war against modern poetry, which evidently is not jolly enough for him either, and takes his place proudly at the side of Bennett Cerf. In the first issue of *Horizon*, he is prepared to dismiss the entire life's work of a man much more serious than he with a gay joke:

> In our language there is quite a large collection of nonsense poetry and of nonsense prose. I do not mean the *Cantos* of Ezra Pound.

We therefore award him **The Blue Toad** on a background of Doric pillars and nursery rhymes.

MEDITATION PAGE

'Freedom is, above all, freedom from lies.'
—*D. H. Lawrence*

'You graduates of West Point are all crusaders for Peace.'
—*Eisenhower*, June 1958.

'The more you buy, the happier you are.'
—*All Advertisers.*

'The fallout from H-bombs is no more dangerous than a radium wrist-watch.'
—*Teller.*

'Soap operas give the people what they want.'
—*Defense-Secretary McElroy.*

'We only exploded 12 bombs in the recent tests.'
—*The Pentagon.*

'Going to church is good business.'
—*Sunday School.*

GOTTFRIED BENN

GOTTFRIED BENN was considered the greatest poet in Germany on his death in 1956. Like William Carlos Williams he was a doctor all his life, but unlike Williams, he was as interested in the inner life as in the outer world. He writes mainly two kinds of poems, pleasant and unpleasant. In the unpleasant poems, he is, as every doctor learns to be, very out-spoken about disease; his first book of poems was called *Morgue*.

With Munch he was a founder of Expressionism, in which they used everything and whatever they could see in the world, trees, bridges, faces, in any way possible to express the new emotions they felt moving within themselves. As Munch said, 'My work is to paint pictures of the modern soul-life'.

Benn, in the generation of the Tens, was an exile from Hitler when he was about forty-five years old; on his return to Germany after the War, he announced what he called the Second Phase of Expressionism, which is still considered the major movement in German literature after the War, and of which the poems here are a part. He felt that what could be gained by busy-ness, activity, was at an end, and he felt we should move toward solitude, aloneness, stillness, and his book in 1947 was called *Poems That Stand Still*, of which we have the title poem here. The idea of 'standing still' or 'motionlessness' also intends a sort of poetic opposition to Berthold Brecht, whose poems always have a great deal of motion, usually toward revolution.

During the course of his life, Benn became interested in a new movement of the imagination within a poem. This movement of the imagination results in a poem which, as I understand it, is not arranged in layers, like the old poem, the sonnet, for instance, but differently. The images of this new poem are not a series of arguments following each other, but groups of images which come to the poem like birds to a tree, or which arrange themselves about a hidden core. The poems, *Ah, That Land So Far Off*, and *Poems That Stand Still*, translated here, are both good examples of that kind of poem, I think, a poem of images, which Benn simply referred to as having the 'orangenstil', the structure of an orange.

JUAN RAMÓN JIMÉNEZ

WE ARE PROUD TO PUBLISH here the translations of Jiménez by Carlos de Francisco Zea. They are the best of the translations of Jiménez done so far; they are, for instance, the only ones which carry over into the translation his delicacy and enthusiasm. It is only in reading these translations for the first time that the subject matter of Jiménez becomes clear: he does not write of politics or religious doctrines, of the mistakes of others, not of his own fancies or even his own opinions, but only of solitude, and the strange experiences and the strange joy that come to a man in solitude.

In solitude a man's emotions become very clear to him, and Jiménez' books usually consist of emotion after emotion called out with great force and delicacy, and it must be said that his short, precise poems make our tradition of the long egotistic ode look rather absurd. Seeing the beauty of a sunset, for instance, he does not, with many stanzas, complicated syntax, and involved thoughts, write a long elaborate ode on immortality; he simply says:

> Serene last evening,
> Short as a life,
> End of all that was loved,
> I want to be eternal!

This is what he calls 'naked poetry'. It is poetry near the emotion. He has a wonderful poem in which he says that, in his youth, when poetry first came to him, she came to him like a very young girl, naked, and he loved her. Then, later, she began to put on ornaments and become very elaborate, and he began to hate her, without knowing why. Then, years later, she began to trust him, and now, at last is a young girl, naked again—'O naked poetry, my lifelong passion!'

Jiménez, as a poet, was born in the great and joyful reviving of Spanish poetry about 1905, led by Antonio Machado,

Unamuno, and others, who dreamed of a 'new blossoming of Spain'. In 1916, Jiménez came to the United States for the first time to marry his wife, Zenobia, who was the sister of a man who owned a Spanish-American newspaper in New York; there is an interesting poem from that time called something like: 'In a room on Washington Square, with my bags all packed, I wait to leave.' In the Thirties, when Franco won, all the poets of that magnificent spring became exiles, except Lorca who was killed by Franco during the war, and Miguel Hernandez, in Robert Lowell's generation, whom Franco starved to death in a prison about 1947. With Rafael Alberti, Jorge Guillen, Pedro Salinas, Emilio Prados, Manuel Altolaguirre, Luis Cernuda, and other fine poets, Jiménez went into exile. He spent most of his exile in Puerto Rico, part in Washington. Franco asked him to return to Spain, after he won the Nobel Prize, but he refused.

His love for his wife was one of the greatest devotions of his life, and he wrote many of his poems for her. When he received the Nobel Prize in 1956, his wife was on her deathbed, and he told the reporters to go away, would not go to Stockholm, said his wife should have gotten the Nobel Prize, and that he was no longer interested. After his wife died, he did not write another poem, and died a few months later, in the spring of 1958.

AMERICAN CONTRIBUTORS

JAMES WRIGHT decided this spring to abandon what he calls 'nineteenth century poetry', and the poems printed here are the first he has written in his new manner. He writes us that his interest in the new poetry began years ago, when wandering by mistake into the wrong classroom in Vienna, he heard an old professor talk with great excitement of Georg Trakl. Mr. Wright was Yale Younger Series poet in 1957, with strictly 'classical' poems, and has another book of the same type coming out in September with Wesleyan. He was born in Martin's Ferry, Ohio, one of the little Ohio river towns near the great steel mills, and he says one of the strangest experiences of his life was his first reading, as a child, of the Blake line: 'The Ohio shall wash my stains from me'.

THOMAS PARNELL is from West Virginia. After service with the United States Marine Corps in World War II, he went to France, where he has lived for a number of years. He published a small book of poems there called *The Auctioneer*. In the fall of 1957, he returned to the United States and is now working in Washington.

CARLOS DE FRANCISCO ZEA was born in Columbia. He has lived since in several other Latin-American countries, including Mexico, and is now living in the United States, in Chicago. He writes: 'Although I am majoring in biology at the University of Chicago, my interest in the humanities, particularly in German poetry, is just as great as in the sciences.' The translations here are the first translations of Jiménez he has published, but to the great interest of the editors, he is preparing an entire book of translations from Jiménez which will cover his poetical work from 1898 to the early 1950's.

EDITH DESORT, who has done the fine translation of Benn's 'Lebe Wohl—', was born in Chicago in 1934, and lives there still. She is thinking of making a profession of translating. She writes: 'I hope to concentrate all efforts of translation upon the late 19th and 20th century literature; this would include Büchner, Wedekind, Kleist, Hofmannsthal, Borchert, Rilke, and Benn. But it is the imagination and spirit of Herman Hesse which I feel is most needed now. Then, if a "breakthrough" of a new literary generation in Germany occurs, I will work only on that.' She is at present a student.

ABEDNEGO is a young poet now at the University of Michigan. We invite more short notes of this kind.